Dear Parent,

In <u>What Is a Butterfly?</u> your
will learn about the lif
a butterfly. Squirrel
Christopher and his fr
erpillar, who explains ea
his life. Turn the page to
what happens in each stage.

Sincerely,

Rita D. Gaula

Managing Editor

FAMILY FUN

- Help your child find chrysalides on
  trees and bushes in your backyard or
  take your child to a local park to find
  them. Keep each chrysalis in a large
  covered glass jar with air holes
  punched in the lid. When the butterfly hatches, be sure your
  child sets it free.

READ MORE ABOUT IT

- *Why Do Birds Fly South?*

This book is a presentation of Weekly Reader
Books. Weekly Reader Books offers book
clubs for children from preschool through high
school. For further information write to:
WEEKLY READER BOOKS, 4343 Equity Drive,
Columbus, Ohio 43228

This edition is published by arrangement
with Checkerboard Press.

Weekly Reader is a federally registered trademark
of Field Publications.

WEEKLY READER BOOKS presents

What Is a Butterfly?

A **Just Ask**™ Book

Hi, my name is
Christopher!

by Chris Arvetis
and Carole Palmer

illustrated by
Jim Conahan

FIELD PUBLICATIONS
MIDDLETOWN, CT.

Caterpillar !

Look at the eggs on this leaf.
Many of these eggs will hatch.
When an egg hatches, a tiny
caterpillar crawls out.

Amazing!

Look!
There is an egg hatching.
See the tiny caterpillar
coming out.

Look!

There are many kinds
of caterpillars.
Some are very colorful.
Let me tell you more
about caterpillars.

A caterpillar's body is made up of 14 parts, including the head.

The parts are called segments. SEG-MENTS.

A caterpillar's head has eyes and a pair of feelers.

It has a mouth and strong jaws for biting.

14 parts!

Below a caterpillar's mouth
is a part called a spinneret.
SPIN-NER-ET.
Something that looks like water
comes out through the spinneret.
It quickly hardens into a material
that looks like string.
The string helps the caterpillar
stick to whatever it is crawling on.

Interesting !

A caterpillar's body
can be smooth.

It can also be covered
with hair.

A caterpillar has
lots of legs, too.

A caterpillar grows,
but its skin does not.

When a caterpillar gets
too big, its skin splits.

The skin splits near the
caterpillar's head and
down its back.

The caterpillar crawls
out of the old skin.

Now it wears new skin.

This happens over and over
as the caterpillar grows.

Over and over!

Finally the caterpillar grows as big as it will be.

When this happens, it is ready for its next stage.

While hanging quietly from a twig or leaf, the caterpillar's skin splits for the last time.

The skin falls off.

Next, a hard shell called a chrysalis covers the caterpillar's body.

Can you say CHRYS-A-LIS?

CHRYS-A-LIS!

That's a chrysalis!

Now the chrysalis starts
to turn into a butterfly.
Wings start to form.
So do eyes and long feelers.
All but six legs disappear.

About two weeks later,
the chrysalis splits and
the butterfly crawls out.

At first, its body
and wings are soft.

But before long,
they become strong.

CHRYSALIS

CATERPILLAR

EGG

BUTTERFLY

A butterfly starts from an egg, becomes a caterpillar, then a chrysalis, and finally a full-grown butterfly.